Sam and the Fish

by Katrina Davino • illustrated by John Lund

Lucy Calkins and Michael Rae-Grant, Series Editors

LETTER-SOUND CORRESPONDENCES

m, t, a, n, s, ss, p, i, d, g, o, c, k, ck, r, u, h, b, e, f, ff, l, ll, z, j, v, **w**

HIGH-FREQUENCY WORDS

is, like, see, the, no, so, as, his, too, of, go, to, for, look, he, **was**

Sam and the Fish
Author: Katrina Davino
Series Editors: Lucy Calkins and Michael Rae-Grant

Heinemann
145 Maplewood Avenue, Suite 300
Portsmouth, NH 03801
www.heinemann.com

Cataloging-in-Publication data is on file with the Library of Congress.

ISBN-13: 978-0-325-13820-6

Design and Production: Dinardo Design LLC, Carole Berg, and Rebecca Anderson

Editors: Anna Cockerille and Jennifer McKenna

Illustrations: John Lund

Photographs: p. 32 (fishing boat) © cybercrisi/Shutterstock; inside back cover (girl in rain) © Yuganov Konstantin/Shutterstock; inside back cover (girl in wig) © Just dance /Shutterstock.

Manufacturing: Gerard Clancy

Printed in Dongguan, China
4 5 6 7 8 9 10 TP 28 27 26 25 24 23
April 2023 Printing / PO# 4500868396

Contents

Meet...

Sam Dad Mom

Em Jon Kat

Get In, Sam!

It is hot.

So Mom and Dad and the kids
go to a pond.

Mom and Dad get in.

Em and Jon and Kat get in.

But Sam will not get in.

5

The sun IS hot.

So Dad gets a sun hat for Sam.

7

9

Dad zips up the vest...

and Sam gets in at last!

The Big Fish

Mom and Dad set up rigs
for the fish.
Sam dips his rig in the pond.

Sam sits.

The kids sit.

Mom and Dad sit.

The sun is so, so hot.

And no fish nip at the rigs.

Until...

The kids sit up.

Was it a fish?

It was! A fish bit the rig!

The kids see it in the pond.

Dad helps Sam tug it in.

It is a big, fat fish!

The fish swims

into the web of the net.

The fish wags in the net,
and the kids get wet!

The kids look at the fish.

It looks a bit sad.

Mom plops the fish
back in the pond,
and it swims off.

Was It a Cod?

Sam looks for his fish.

He flips past clams and crabs.

Was it a cod?

A cod is a fast fish,

and his fish was fast too...

but it was not tan like a cod.

Was it a sun fish?

No, no, no.

It was not as big as a sun fish!

Sam flips past a lot of fish.

Was it a cat fish?

No, it did not look like a cat fish.

Was it a bass? Well...

The fish had fat lips like a bass.
And the fish swam in a pond
like a bass. So...

31

FISHING

People all over the world go fishing for fun. One time, a man named Alfred Dean went fishing, and he caught a fish that weighed 2,664 pounds. That's about as much as a car! It is the biggest fish anyone has ever caught.

Some people go fishing because it's their job. They're called *commercial fishers*. When they catch a fish, they sell it in a market, or in a grocery or restaurant. Sometimes commercial fishers catch fish with big nets instead of fishing rods. They drag the net through the water and scoop up hundreds of fish all at once. When they drag the net like that, it's called *trawling*. Commercial fishers have to be careful when they go trawling because if they catch too many fish, it's not good for the ocean!

Talk about...

Ask your reader some questions like...

- What happened in this book?

- Why didn't Sam want to get in the boat at first? What was he worried about?

- Why do you think Sam and his family decided to let the fish go?

- Would you want to go fishing? Why?